Hammerhead Sharks

BY ALLAN MOREY

AMICUS HIGH INTEREST • AMICUS INK

Amicus High Interest and Amicus Ink are imprints of Amicus
P.O. Box 1329, Mankato, MN 56002
www.amicuspublishing.us

Library of Congress Cataloging-in-Publication Data
Morey, Allan, author.
Hammerhead sharks / by Allan Morey.
    pages cm. – (Sharks)
Audience: K to grade 3.
Includes bibliographical references and index.
ISBN 978-1-60753-978-0 (library binding)
ISBN 978-1-68152-091-9 (pbk.)
ISBN 978-1-68151-012-5 (ebook)
1. Hammerhead sharks–Juvenile literature. 2. Sharks–Juvenile
literature. I. Title.
QL638.95.S7M67 2017
597.3–dc23

                              2015033750

Editor: Wendy Dieker
Series Designer: Kathleen Petelinsek
Book Designer: Aubrey Harper
Photo Researcher: Rebecca Bernin

Photo Credits: Martin Strmiska / Alamy cover, 5; Michael
Weberberger/imageBROKER/Corbis 6; SeaPics 9;
imageBROKER / Alamy 10-11; qldian / iStock 13; Martin
Strmiska / Alamy 14; imageBROKER / Alamy 17; Martin
Strmiska / Alamy 18; Jeff Rotman / Getty 21; frantisekhojdysz
/ Shutterstock 22; Martin Strmiska / Alamy 24-25; SeaPics 26;
David Fleetham / OceanwideImages.com 29

Printed in the United States of America.

HC 10 9 8 7 6 5 4 3 2 1
PB 10 9 8 7 6 5 4 3 2 1

Table of Contents

Ocean Hunter

A dark shape swims through the water. It is a shark looking for food. This shark has a wide head. As it swims, its head moves back and forth. It looks like a swinging hammer. The hammerhead shark sees its **prey**. It darts after a fish. Water swirls. Teeth gnash. Chomp!

These hammerheads are swinging their heads back and forth. They are looking for fish to eat.

The great hammerhead is the largest kind of hammerhead.

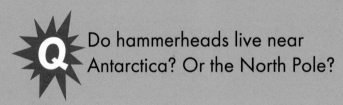 Do hammerheads live near Antarctica? Or the North Pole?

6

Nine kinds of hammerheads swim in the ocean. The great hammerhead is the biggest. It grows up to 20 feet (6 m). The bonnethead is one of the smallest. It is only 2 to 3 feet (0.6 to 1 m) long.

Hammerheads swim in warm places. They stay mostly in shallow water. They swim off the coasts of almost all the continents.

 No. It is too cold in those places.

Not all hammerheads look the same.
You can tell some apart by the shape of
their heads. The winghead has a very
wide head. It can be 3 feet (1 m) wide. A
bonnethead has a narrow head. It looks
more like a shovel than a hammer. The
scalloped hammerhead has round ridges on
its head.

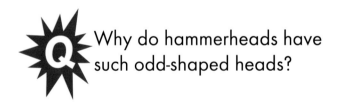
Q Why do hammerheads have such odd-shaped heads?

This bonnethead has a narrower head than other hammerheads.

 It is a mystery! Scientists are not sure.

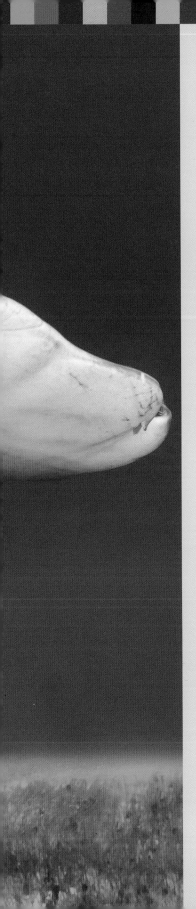

Dinner Time

Hammerheads often hunt at night by themselves. They will eat almost anything. They snack on **bony fish**. These include sardines, herring, and boxfish. They catch squid, shrimp, and crabs. Hammerheads even gulp down smaller hammerheads!

Chomp! This shark found prey to snack on.

A great hammerhead is a fierce **predator**. Its favorite meal is stingray. But a stingray can be dangerous. It has **venomous** spines on its tail. If a person gets stung— ouch! It hurts. That is not true for hammerheads. The sting does not hurt them. They eat the stingray whole. That includes the spines.

Some predators see this stingray and keep away. Hammerheads see food!

We don't know why this shark has such an odd head. But we do know it helps them see really well.

 Can hammerheads smell?

Hammerheads are great hunters. One reason is because of their wide heads. Their eyes are on the sides of their heads. With a small twist of their bodies, they can see all around them. That helps them find food. Their eyes are also spread apart. This helps them see how far away their prey is.

 Yes! They can smell just a tiny drop of blood in a large pool of water. That means lunch!

Sharks can sense things that people cannot. On their **snouts** are special sensors. They can feel electricity in the water. When animals move, they give off tiny bits of energy. Then sharks can tell where their prey is.

The hammerhead's wide snout has more sensors than other sharks. They can even find a stingray hidden in the sand.

Do other animals have these kinds of sensors?

Look at this wide snout! It is full of sensors that can feel other animals moving nearby.

 Yes, stingrays do too. They are cousins to sharks.

These scalloped hammerheads gather together. Maybe some will find mates.

Life Cycle

During the day, hammerhead sharks gather in schools. There may be hundreds in a school. In schools, they find a mate.
A female hammerhead gives birth about 11 months after mating. She gives **live birth** to her young. Young sharks are called pups. There are up to 40 pups in a **litter**.

Pups look like tiny **adults**. They can swim. They can find food on their own. And they need to! Adult hammerheads do not take care of their young. Grown sharks might even eat pups for a snack.

Pups stay close to shore where it is safe from big fish. As they grow larger, they swim farther out to sea.

 How long do hammerheads live?

This pup doesn't have protection from its mother. It is born ready to take care of itself.

 Up to 30 years.

Hammerheads swim without fear. They are the hunters of the ocean.

Life as a Hunter

No other animals hunt large hammerhead sharks. But that is not true for small hammerheads or pups. They can be a meal for larger sharks.

A hammerhead's coloring helps it sneak up on its food. From below, it is hard to see. It has a light-colored belly. This color blends in with the light shining down from above.

Hammerheads are great swimmers. They can twist their bodies. They can turn sharply. They can dart quickly through the water. These abilities help them catch fish.

Some people think their odd-shaped heads help them swim. Their heads kind of look like an airplane wing. They may work like one too. Their heads might help them swim up through the water.

This shark's strong body can twist and turn quickly.

**Divers work to cut a dead
shark out of a fishing net.**

Sharks and People

A great hammerhead shark might be dangerous. But that is only because of its large size. Attacks are rare. Most sharks stay away from people.

People cause more danger to sharks. Hammerheads die when they get caught in fishing nets. People also try to catch for them for food. They are used to make shark fin soup.

Hammerheads need to be protected. Some are in danger of going **extinct**. This is true for the scalloped hammerhead. Some governments are working to keep hammerheads safe. They have passed new laws. These laws make it a crime to fish for hammerheads. They will make sure these odd-looking sharks keep swimming in the world's oceans.

This scalloped hammerhead can live a long life if people work to help them survive.

Glossary

adult A fully mature animal.

bony fish Fish with skeletons, such as catfish and sardines.

coast Land near the edge of the water.

extinct No longer existing in the world.

litter A group of young animals.

live birth When young animals are born from a mother's body; not hatched from eggs.

predator An animal that eats other animals.

prey Animals eaten as food by other animals.

snout The part of the face where the nose and mouth are.

venomous Poisonous; able to inject a venom by biting or stinging.

Read More

Franchino, Vicky. *Hammerhead Sharks*. New York: Children's Press, an imprint of Scholastic Inc., 2015.

Magby, Meryl. *Hammerhead Sharks*. New York: PowerKids Press, 2013.

Musgrave, Ruth. *National Geographic Kids Everything Sharks*. Washington, D.C.: National Geographic, 2011.

Websites

A-Z Animals: Hammerhead Sharks
a-z-animals.com/animals/hammerhead-shark

Kid Zone: Shark Facts
www.kidzone.ws/sharks/facts.htm

National Geographic Kids: Hammerhead Sharks
kids.nationalgeographic.com/animals/hammerhead-shark

Index

About the Author

Allan Morey is a children's book author and animal lover. He's had pet fish, birds, ferrets, pigs, cats, and dogs. Animals are one of his favorite subjects to write about. He now lives in St. Paul, Minnesota, with his wife, two kids, and dog, Ty.